NICK FAWCETT

Touched by His Hand

Prayers for Daily Life

Augsburg Books
MINNEAPOLIS

TOUCHED BY HIS HAND
Prayers for Daily Life

Copyright © 2005 Nick Fawcett
Original edition published in English under
the title TOUCHED BY HIS HAND by
Kevin Mayhew Ltd, Buxhall, England.
This edition copyright © Fortress Press 2019

All rights reserved. Except for brief quotations in critical articles or reviews, no part of this book may be reproduced in any manner without prior written permission from the publisher. Email copyright@augsburgfortress.org or write to Permissions, Fortress Press, PO Box 1209, Minneapolis, MN 55440-1209.

Cover image: Cover photo by Chainarong Prasertthai from iStock
Cover design: Alisha Lofgren

Print ISBN: 978-1-5064-5967-7

Contents

Introduction   7

1   The Rugby Team   9
2   The Soccer Match   10
3   The Engine Tune-Up   11
4   The Gym   12
5   The Production Line   13
6   The Home Improvement Store   14
7   The Traffic Lights   15
8   The Pay Stub   16
9   The Hospital   17
10 The Blood Donation   18
11 The Weather Forecast   19
12 The Morning Shave   20
13 The Traffic Cop   21
14 The Makeover   22
15 The Pool Player   23
16 The Television   24
17 The Beach   25
18 The Internet   26
19 The Photo Album   27
20 The Suitcase   28
21 The Loose Connection   29
22 The Binge-Drinkers   30
23 The Doctor's Waiting Room   31
24 The Camera   32
25 The Hairdressers   33
26 The Hot Shower   34
27 The Newspaper   35
28 The River   36
29 The Fast-Food Restaurant   37
30 The Fuse   38
31 The Fish Tank   39

32	The Sea Stack	40
33	The Legal Document	41
34	The Vending Machine	42
35	The City Park	43
36	The Garden	44
37	The Identical Twins	45
38	The Wall	46
39	The Pen	47
40	The Convenience Store	48
41	The Round of Drinks	49
42	The Stretcher	50
43	The Seagull	51
44	The Bluebell Woods	52
45	The Antiques Dealer	53
46	The Injury	54
47	The Garbage Collection	55
48	The Abortion Clinic	56
49	The Charity Collector	58
50	The Dictionary	59
51	The Time	60
52	The Cul-De-Sac	61
53	The AIDS Sufferer	62
54	The Rechargeable Battery	63
55	The Pebble	64
56	The Breeze	65
57	The Text Message	66
58	The Baby	67
59	The Toddler	68
60	The Discarded Lottery Ticket	69
61	The Advertisements	70
62	The Fisherman	71
63	The Supermarket	72
64	The Oak Tree	73
65	The Politician	74
66	The eBay Auction	75
67	The Footprints	76
68	The Meal	77

69	The Computer Scan	78
70	The Tide	79
71	The Vacation	80
72	The Street Cleaner	81
73	The Muslim	82
74	The Calculator	83
75	The Space Probe	84
76	The New Home	85
77	The Moving Truck	86
78	The Sunglasses	87
79	The Movie Theater	88
80	The Accident	89
81	The Military Graves	90
82	The Credit Card Statement	91
83	The Door	92
84	The Footpath	93
85	The Hall of Mirrors	94
86	The Fountain	95
87	The Ruler	96
88	The Stain	97
89	The Shoelaces	98
90	The Chapel of Rest	99
91	The Bananas	100
92	The Storm Clouds	101
93	The Ecstasy Tablet	102
94	The Medicine	103
95	The Surfers	104
96	The Jigsaw Puzzle	105
97	The Bridge	106
98	The Swimming Lesson	107
99	The Wrong Note	108
100	The Ornament	109

*To Jackie and Mike,
a dear sister and brother-in-law,
and an inspiration to so many*

Introduction

Years ago, in his book *Prayers of Life*, the celebrated Christian writer Michel Quoist wrote of all life becoming a prayer, everything we see, hear, think, and feel being touched by God's presence. That idea has lived with me ever since—a goal I have striven toward realizing, though rarely attained. Instead of being a specifically religious activity divorced from daily life, talking with God—which, after all, is what prayer is all about—should be integral to each day, arising naturally from the people, places, experiences, and events that are part of it.

Unfortunately, matters aren't quite that straightforward, for the gulf between heaven and earth is such that we can lose sight of any contact between the two. Indeed, so strong is the hold this world exerts on us that it frequently obscures the spiritual dimension to life altogether, to the point that God is crowded out, all but forgotten. We rely on times of devotion—whether privately or in fellowship with others—to rekindle a sense of his presence and restore our broken relationship, yet in doing so we unconsciously perpetuate the divide between the sacred and secular, divine and human.

This book attempts to offer a way out of the impasse. Avoiding religious jargon as far as possible, and resisting the temptation to link prayers to particular passages of Scripture—easy though this would be in most cases—it comprises a hundred prayers rooted in everyday life. The commonplace provides a backdrop to the holy, to a living encounter with God: a pay stub, television, camera, or lottery ticket; a traffic cop or pool player; a beach, river, garden, or fountain; even a bunch of bananas—each can be seen as in some way pointing to his presence and involvement in the daily routine. They may, of course, speak very differently to you than to me, but the point is that even the most ordinary aspect of life can and does speak of God if we are open to listen and respond, each one, to the eye of faith, being touched by his hand. My hope, in writing this book, is that something in its pages will help bring home that truth, so that life—if not entirely, then at least a little—may become more fully a prayer.

NICK FAWCETT

1
The Rugby Team

His teammates engulfed him,
    leaping and laughing,
    sharing his jubilation as he punched the air in triumph,
    delight on his face.
The try was his,
    but the moment owned by all,
    for each had contributed,
    if not to the move itself then in the play earlier.
The clever shimmy,
    last-ditch tackle,
    defense-splitting pass,
    bruising scrum—
    each had added to the whole,
    the game not about one but many.

Teach me, Lord, that I need others,
    just as they need me;
    that life is interconnected,
    what I owe balanced by what I can contribute.
Whether I'm the center of attention or unnoticed,
    help me to play my part,
    working both *with* and *for* others
    to the common good.
Amen.

2
The Soccer Match

He should have passed—
    one simple ball to the man in space,
    and a goal was all but certain.
He knew it,
    the fans knew it,
    even the ref knew it,
    but he'd carried on—
    eyes only for personal glory—
    and the crowd groaned,
    teammates cursed,
    as he took on one player too many . . .
    and squandered the chance.

Lord, in pursuing personal goals and ambitions,
    teach me to think also of others,
    and, where necessary, to put their interests
    before my own.
Give me the humility I need
    to take a back seat sometimes,
    play a supporting part,
    and let others enjoy their moment.
Amen.

3
The Engine Tune-Up

It wasn't complicated—
    just a change of oil, sparkplugs, air filter, and so forth—
    but the impact was dramatic,
    my old junker suddenly a limousine:
    engine steady,
    acceleration smooth,
    handling responsive.

Lord, overhaul my life,
    and make me new.
Recharge my batteries
    and clear away whatever prevents me
    from realizing my true potential.
So work within me that I may not just get by,
    but live each moment to the full.
Amen.

4
The Gym

They were a mixed bunch—
    some fighting the flab,
    subjecting protesting bodies to unaccustomed exertion;
    others young and athletic,
    cultivating bulging biceps and body beautiful—
    but they shared a common cause:
    the pursuit of physical health.

Lord, I don't want to neglect my body,
    for it is your gift,
    but what of my soul,
    the inner self?
Teach me to seek wholeness of spirit with equal resolve,
    to work for true well-being,
    to cultivate health that will neither fade nor perish.
Amen.

5
The Production Line

They came off the conveyor belt one after the other,
   hour after hour,
   day after day—
   the same process,
   the same result,
   each a soulless copy of the one before,
   an automated clone.

Save us, Lord,
   as individuals or a society,
   from treating people the same way,
   seeing them as objects to be exploited,
   statistics processed,
   consumers targeted,
   resources managed.
Remind us that in your eyes
   we are all unique and precious,
   valued for who we are—
   each seen not as an object
   but as a person.
Help us, then, in our dealings with others,
   to see behind the labels
   and to recognize the intrinsic worth of all.
Amen.

6
The Home Improvement Store

I walked among the shelves, Lord—
  row upon row of tools, machinery, and equipment—
  and they conjured up such contrasting pictures:
  skilled craftsmen surveying a job well done . . .
  and ham-fisted amateurs regretting a job botched;
  homes improved . . .
  and houses ruined,
  creative triumphs . . .
  and DIY disasters.

Like everyone, Lord, I can do *some* things by myself,
  but not all,
    for as well as strengths I have weaknesses,
    as well as skills, deficiencies.
Teach me to know which is which:
  to tackle what I *can* do
  but admit to what I *can't*.
Amen.

7
The Traffic Lights

I put my foot down,
   determined to beat the lights,
   but they changed as I approached,
   forcing me to brake,
   and I seethed in frustration,
   bemoaning my luck.

Why, Lord?
What did I hope to gain?
Why did I sour the day in search of a few seconds more?
Grant me the gift of patience
   and the ability to celebrate each moment,
   whatever it may bring.
Teach me to savor the here and now,
   and to let go of what might be or could have been.
Amen.

8
The Pay Stub

It spoke, that pay stub:
    of work done and leisure made possible,
    of food on the table and clothes for the kids,
    of presents, treats, vacations, and outings,
    the mortgage and new car,
    taxes paid and retirement contributions—
    all this and so much more.
It spoke too of those with no wage:
    the unemployed,
    asylum seekers,
    refugees,
    millions the world over condemned to poverty
    and a life of need.

I don't earn much, Lord—
    a mere pittance compared to some—
    but it's a king's ransom to others,
    riches beyond their wildest dreams.
However much, then, I may strive for more,
    teach me first to appreciate what I have,
    and gratefully to respond to those with so much less.
Amen.

9
The Hospital

I walked through the maze of corridors,
    searching for the right ward,
    and behind the stark labels that greeted me—
    oncology department,
    men's health,
    maternity suite,
    morgue—
    lay a labyrinth of emotions,
    untold individuals waiting and wondering,
    living and dying:
    such hopes, yet such fears;
    such joy, yet such sorrow;
    such relief, yet such pain;
    such healing, yet such brokenness—
    a poignant tapestry of delight and despair.

Hear my prayer, Lord,
    for patients and their loved ones,
    but above all, for those who staff our hospitals—
    those with the courage to face, day after day,
    the sheer intensity of it all,
    striving with such dedication to nurture wholeness
    in body, mind, and spirit.
Thank you for their skill and compassion;
    the renewal they bring,
    life they make possible,
    understanding they show
    and comfort they extend.
Thank you for their willingness to care for others.
Amen.

10
The Blood Donation

They sipped their tea and went home,
   another routine donation,
   unsung,
   unnoticed.
Yet from so simple an offering
   comes so special a gift to so great a multitude:
   the heart-bypass patient and hemorrhaging mother,
   the baby with leukemia and child in intensive care,
   the attempted suicide with severed artery,
   the overdosed teenager,
   hemophiliac,
   crash victim,
   man with blood poisoning
   and woman with anemia—
   just some whose lives are touched each day.

Lord Jesus Christ, who shed your blood for all,
   thank you for those who give theirs to others in turn.
Amen.

11
The Weather Forecast

"Showers dying out from the west,
    followed by sunny intervals with a gentle breeze"—
    isn't that what he said?
It's not what we got, though—
    nothing like it.
It's poured since this morning
    and is still storming now,
    the most we've had just a brief burst of sunshine,
    a tantalizing glimpse of what might have been.

Lord, we can try to plan ahead,
    predict the future,
    and yes, at times, make a decent go of it,
    but in things that really matter,
    life-shaping events and issues,
    we can rarely be confident,
    still less sure.
Teach us that, though we may map our intended path,
    it is you who directs? our steps,
    and you alone who hold the future in your hands.
Amen.

12
The Morning Shave

I stood there, as I'd stood so many times before,
   razor in hand and face lathered,
   and it struck me how many hours, days, weeks
   I must have spent in total
   performing that same repetitive chore,
   year in, year out, for longer than I cared to remember.
What a waste it seemed,
   for how much more I could have done with that time.
But then I paused, and pondered,
   thinking of those for whom a roof over their head
   and basic sanitation,
   let alone a warm house and hot water,
   would be a luxury,
   the stuff of dreams.
I thought of those paralyzed by birth or injury,
   deprived of sight,
   or too infirm to perform even the simplest tasks,
   and I realized how much they'd give
   to swap places at that moment.

Forgive me, Lord, for taking for granted
   the little things of life
   and health that allows me to experience them.
Teach me to celebrate even the simplest of moments,
   however mundane they may seem.
Amen.

13
The Traffic Cop

He moved slowly down the street,
   scribbling in his notebook
   and occasionally issuing a ticket . . .
   and passersby eyed him uneasily,
   a few scurrying anxiously back to their cars,
   looking furtively over their shoulders
   as if they suspected him of giving chase.
For many he was the enemy—
   resented,
   feared,
   loathed—
   but he was just an ordinary person
   doing what he was paid to do,
   and without him chaos would swiftly follow,
   roads dangerously snarled up with traffic,
   everyone the loser.

Lord, I see *you* sometimes as a setter and enforcer of rules,
   and I don't always like obeying them—
   not when they clash with personal gratification
   or demand more of me than I'd like to give—
   yet you give them for my benefit rather than yours,
   so that all can enjoy your blessings
   and live life to the full.
Teach me, then,
   not to fear you as one rigidly imposing law
   but, freely, gladly, and gratefully, to honor your will.
Amen.

14
The Makeover

It was remarkable:
    a touch of lipstick,
    dab of eye shadow,
    new outfit,
    change of hairstyle,
    and she looked a new person,
    unrecognizable from the woman she'd been before.

Lord, it's different, I know,
    but I too am good at putting on appearances,
    looking the part,
    the face I show to the world
    so often concealing the reality beneath.
Help me to change not so much the outside
    but deep within—
    to become the person you would have me be.
Amen.

15
The Pool Player

He made it look so easy,
> rattling in one ball after another,
> and each time the next shot was lined up perfectly,
> the break accumulated with quiet but assured precision.

Only, of course, it *wasn't* easy;
> it was the result of years of discipline,
> countless days practising at the table
> executing those seemingly effortless pots
> time after time,
> until a truly breathtaking skill
> became almost as natural as breathing.

Lord, give me similar commitment in following you,
> similar resolve to honor your will,
> similar dedication in honor.

Teach me truly to practice what I preach,
> in the sense of working at it each day,
> until walking the way of Christ becomes second nature,
> not the exception but the norm.

Amen.

16
The Television

There are so many channels, Lord—
  movies,
  sports,
  history,
  news,
  drama,
  music,
  and discovery,
  not to mention local broadcasts
  and a host of others,
  each clamoring for my attention.

I could watch all of them so easily
  but I don't want to,
  for they're finally about others,
  not me;
  proxy experiences,
  surrogate thoughts and feelings.

I'll watch some programs, of course,
  and enjoy them too—
  nothing wrong with that—
  but save me, Lord, from a secondhand existence;
  from spending too much time
  watching other people's lives
  and not enough living my own.
Amen.

17
The Beach

I ran the sand through my fingers, Lord,
   millions of grains,
   yet that one handful was just a fraction
   of what made up the beach;
   that beach one of thousands across the world,
   and the world itself merely a tiny speck
   in the vastness of space
   with its trillions of constellations
   and plethora of galaxies.

It leaves me reeling, Lord,
   such magnitude truly awesome,
   yet you brought it all into being,
   sustaining it each day,
   and leading it toward fulfillment;
   the universe and everything within it
   the work of your hands.
As you created the stars and the sand,
   so you have fashioned our lives—
   knowing us better than we know ourselves,
   calling us by name,
   loving us more than we can begin to fathom.
For the vastness of your purpose,
   the immensity of your creation
   and the mind-boggling wonder of your grace,
   Lord, thank you.
Amen.

18
The Internet

I went online, Lord,
    and all at once there was a world of information,
    incalculable resources at my fingertips,
    and into the bargain the opportunity to chat to friends,
    play games,
    and share resources;
    to learn,
    talk,
    and interact with people and places across the globe.

I went online again,
    and suddenly there was a world of corruption:
    sickening and vile pornography,
    images of violence and incitements to hatred,
    perverts grooming their prey,
    and scams targeting the unwary—
    the pimp, torturer, child molester, and conman
    stealing slyly into my living room.

Lord, it disturbs me, the Internet,
    for it's too much like *me*,
    too much like *all* of us,
    capable of so much good,
    yet so much evil,
    so much beauty,
    yet so much ugliness.
Nurture whatever enriches our world,
    whatever builds up,
    and purge that which demeans and degrades.
Amen.

19
The Photo Album

It had a melancholy feel,
    the dog-eared pages and faded photographs
    speaking of moments long gone,
    past glories and pleasures, forever tucked away.
But for the retiree poring over her album
    it was more than an epitaph to distant memories;
    it was a living testimony to special times shared,
    precious people loved,
    and countless experiences enjoyed.

I too, Lord, carry my memories with me,
    if not on paper then in my heart—
    so much I have done,
    so many I have known,
    innumerable people, places, sights, and sounds
    that have enriched and enthralled,
    fashioning the person I am today.
For all I have so richly received,
    Lord, thank you.
Amen.

20
The Suitcase

He gasped,
    struggling with the load,
    veins knotted on his brow,
    and sweat dripping down his cheeks—
    his progress like that of a convict
    wrestling with heavy manacles.
Repeatedly he paused to rest,
    stretching aching fingers and weary arms,
    and I feared for him—
    a man his age with such a burden to carry.

Lord, he is not alone,
    for we all carry baggage through life,
    staggering under a burden of guilt,
    a weight of remorse,
    a crushing load of fear.
Yet we have no need,
    for you are ready to carry
    what we can never shoulder alone.
Teach us in turn to let go
    and walk unencumbered,
    trusting that you hold everything,
    even us,
    in the palm of your hand.
Amen.

21
The Loose Connection

It was just a loose wire, that's all,
   nothing major,
   but though everything else was in perfect order,
   that faulty connection spelled problems,
   impeding the flow of current until it was fixed.

Lord, it's the same with me, I'm afraid—
   your Spirit's power too often prevented
   from getting through.
I don't mean it to happen,
   and don't willfully go wrong;
   it's just that I allow little things,
   small distractions,
   to come between us,
   inexorably multiplying,
   until I become detached from you,
   all contact broken,
   and the flow is stopped.
Forgive me, Lord,
   restore the circuit,
   and connect me again.
Amen.

22
The Binge-Drinkers

They spilled out of the nightclub,
   shouting, singing, and swearing,
   some brawling in the street,
   others relieving themselves in store doorways,
   others again bringing up
   what they had so recently swilled down.
Never mind the hangover next morning,
   the stranger in their bed,
   the night in the police cell—
   this was the highlight of their week,
   a great night out.

Lord, to all who seek pleasure through intoxication,
   blotting out perception to fill the void within,
   grant genuine fulfillment.
Pour into their hearts the sparkling wine of your love
   that they may find true life,
   their cup spilling over,
   full to overflowing.
Amen.

23
The Doctor's Waiting Room

Why are they here, Lord?
A bad back, perhaps,
   heavy cold,
   strained muscle?
A bout of indigestion or heavy cough?
Or perhaps something worse,
   more pressing.
An unexplained lump discovered that morning,
   sending an icy chill down the spine?
A diagnosis anxiously awaited,
   spelling relief or panic,
   acquittal or sentence?
A failed pregnancy,
   dreams dashed again?
Calm expressions and averted eyes
   belie the maelstrom beneath,
   each story locked away until, one by one,
   our names are called,
   and, like penitents at confession,
   we enter the sanctum and blurt out all,
   craving absolution.

Lord, for those troubled about their health,
   and those with the responsibility
   of ministering to them,
   grant your help, guidance, and love.
Amen.

24
The Camera

I wanted to preserve the moment, Lord,
    to keep it on film forever
    so that I could relive it again and again.
Only, of course, I couldn't.
Faithful though the picture was,
    the moment was gone,
    life having moved on,
    and nothing would ever recreate it
    quite as it was before.

Lord, teach me to recall the past but not cling to it,
    to understand that life must be lived forward
    rather than backward,
    what *has been* a stepping stone to what is *yet to be*.
Amen.

25
The Hairdressers

What a strange job,
   cutting all that hair,
   head after head,
   day after day.
Do they get bored, I wonder?
They must do,
   but they don't show it,
   just make casual conversation as they snip away.
They're passing the time of day, of course,
   for they don't know me,
   not *really*—
   don't know most of their customers, come to that.

But *you* do, Lord,
   every hair of my head,
   every thought of my mind,
   every aspect of my character—
   nothing hidden from your gaze.
Inside out and back to front,
   you know each one of us,
   and yearn that we might know you too.
For that great truth,
   Lord, I praise you.
Amen.

26
The Hot Shower

I washed gratefully,
 rinsing away the dirt, dust, sweat, and smoke,
 the grittiness from my eyes
 and weariness from my limbs,
 and I felt not just refreshed but clean,
 almost made new.

Lord, with you there's no *almost* about it:
 you wash us from within,
 cleansing the thoughts of the heart,
 transforming and restoring,
 offering a fresh start,
 new beginnings,
 day after day.
Wash me, I pray, in the fountain of your love.
Amen.

27
The Newspaper

I glimpsed the headline emblazoned over the front page—
   sensational stuff!—
   but shrugged indifferently
   and turned aside,
   for it was old hat,
   yesterday's paper,
   news no longer.
What excited once, bores now,
   what was fresh then, is stale now.

I glimpsed the message running through the pages,
   the Word made flesh,
   Christ crucified and risen—
   sensational stuff!—
   but once more I shrugged and turned aside,
   for again it was old hat,
   news no longer.
Only I was wrong,
   for it's as much today's news as yesterday's,
   as alive now as it will ever be,
   news for you,
   for me,
   for everyone.
Lord, keep me ever-enthused,
   ever-excited,
   by what you have done and continue to do,
   through Christ my Lord.
Amen.

28
The River

It surged past me,
    a mighty torrent,
    and I marvelled at the flow of water,
    at how, year in, year out,
    century after century,
    despite days without rain,
    even weeks of drought,
    it never ran dry.

It spoke of you, Lord:
    your faithful provision and constant love.
Through sunshine and storm,
    summer or winter,
    it remains the same—
    a stream of living water,
    refreshing and reviving,
    unfailing,
    come what may.
For the constancy of that provision,
    receive my praise.
Amen.

29
The Fast-Food Restaurant

There was no shortage of customers:
    morning, afternoon, and evening
    they piled through the doors,
    the mountain of debris they left behind
    testimony to their appetite.
And why not,
    for it was cheap, tasty, and convenient,
    though as for nutrition,
    best not to ask.

I'm good at feeding my body, Lord,
    if careless sometimes what I eat,
    but when it comes to my soul it's a sorrier tale.
Turning my back on food that satisfies—
    living bread,
    true sustenance—
    I cram it instead with junk food,
    a diet that, instead of nourishing, undermines health,
    leaving me spiritually flabby,
    inwardly weak.
Forgive me,
    and teach me to feast at your table
    instead of snacking on empty morsels.
Amen.

30
The Fuse

I should have known better, of course,
   for the lead was never designed for such a load,
   but I kept on adding to it,
   first one plug,
   then another,
   until it became too much
   and the fuse blew.

Lord, that happens with *me*, I'm afraid,
   and sadly with less cause.
Silly little things,
   trivial,
   incidental,
   get me ludicrously worked up
   until sparks fly and I also, so to speak, blow a fuse—
   only in my case it pops too late,
   the explosion of energy wreaking havoc
   before it is spent,
   potentially scarring for life.
Teach me, Lord, when anger takes hold
   to trip the switch before the damage is done.
Amen.

31
The Fish Tank

They darted this way and that,
    probing, foraging, and exploring,
    secure in their own little world.
Were they aware of me looking in,
    conscious of another plane,
    an altogether different dimension,
    beyond the boundaries that confined them?

There's so much, Lord, that *I* don't see,
    the world of my senses not the whole story
    but just a glimpse of reality,
    one aspect of a greater whole.
Save me from being bound by my limited horizons,
    closing my life to wonders beyond
    and riches yet to be revealed.
Open my heart to your infinite love,
    greater than eye has seen or mind conceived.
Amen.

32
The Sea Stack

It looked so solid,
   so permanent,
   standing tall and proud against the waves,
   certain to be there still when I am long gone,
   defying the march of time.
But all was not as it seemed,
   for that rock—
   once a cliff,
   once a mountain—
   was destined to become a boulder,
   pebble,
   stone,
   and, finally, a grain of sand,
   before, who could say, being thrust up again
   in eons to come,
   the whole process beginning again.

Only you, Lord, do not change,
   your love eternal,
   your mercy constant,
   your purpose enduring.
Teach me in this shifting world,
   here today and gone tomorrow,
   to trust in you,
   the same now and always.
Amen.

33
The Legal Document

I read it through,
   and read it again,
   but was none the wiser when I finished
   than when I started.
It was gobbledegook,
   unmitigated jargon,
   no doubt meaning something to someone somewhere,
   but to the ordinary person in the street,
   someone like me,
   conveying nothing.

Lord, do *I* sound like that when I speak of you?
Are the terms I use any easier to understand,
   any more anchored in daily life?
Do I even know what I'm trying to say myself?
So often I use words unthinkingly,
   repeating parrot-fashion what I've heard from others,
   spouting pretentious clichés,
   pious nonsense.
Teach me, rather than simply talking,
   to talk simply.
Amen.

34
The Vending Machine

Tea,
   coffee,
   soup,
   chocolate—
   just a small selection of the drinks on offer.
Insert coins . . .
   select option . . .
   wait.

Lord, I treat *you* like a vending machine sometimes,
   as if all I have to do is press the right buttons
   and you will pander to my wishes.
A drop of devotion and touch of faith,
   with a hint of penitence thrown in,
   and you're bound to come up with the goods,
   whatever I may ask.
Forgive me for seeking to exploit rather than worship you,
   and teach me to focus on what I can give
   instead of dwelling on what I might receive.
Amen.

35
The City Park

It was such a surprise:
    there, so close to the roar of traffic and milling crowds,
    the jostling skyscrapers and throb of city life,
    a little park,
    an oasis of tranquillity,
    a quiet retreat from the hectic world beyond.
Flowers bloomed,
    trees blossomed,
    birds sang,
    squirrels played,
    oblivious to the incongruity of it all.

The peace you promise, Lord, is equally unlikely,
    yet just as real—
    not removed from this world,
    but found amid the hustle and bustle of life,
    the stresses and strains of the daily routine.
Open my heart, Lord,
    to that special peace beyond understanding,
    and may it touch each moment of every day.
Amen.

36
The Garden

I sowed,
   planted,
   weeded,
   pruned,
   and watched in delight as bloom followed bloom
   in a vibrant fusion
   of fragrance and color.

The labor was mine, Lord,
   but the creation yours,
   for it is your hands that fashion such beauty
   and sustain life itself.
Teach me to work in partnership with you,
   not just in the world of plants
   but in the world of everyday life and relationships,
   seeking to nurture the full potential of everyone
   and everything.
Amen.

37
The Identical Twins

You couldn't tell them apart,
>   each the spitting image of the other
>   in build,
>   features,
>   even the expressions they wore.

Differences there must have been,
>   but to my mind they were identical,
>   like peas in a pod,
>   two of a kind.

Lord, no one will ever confuse you and me,
>   but help me at least to resemble you:
>   not in outward appearance,
>   but in the person I am,
>   the things I think and feel, say and do.

Poor though the likeness will always be,
>   may something in my life speak of you,
>   reminding others of the love and care you have for all.

Amen.

38
The Wall

It rose before me,
    high and imposing,
    built to withstand the ravages of time,
    its solid bulk somehow reassuring,
    suggestive of security and permanence
    in an ever-shifting world.
Yet what now was one had once been many—
    a heap of bricks, sand, and cement,
    each of no consequence until they were assembled,
    the one supporting the other—
    weak alone but strong together.

Teach me, Lord, that I too need others—
    that you created me not to exist in isolation
    but to enjoy company,
    interacting with those around me.
Cement, then, the ties of friendship,
    and build up the relationships I share,
    for it is so often through these
    that you give shape and purpose to life.
Amen.

39
The Pen

I found it in the street,
    a cheap ballpoint casually tossed aside,
    the ink having run dry.
I handled it respectfully,
    mindful of the words it had helped to form
    and thoughts convey,
    able to heal or hurt,
    delight or dismay—
    a few simple strokes,
    yielding so much good or so much evil.

Lord, whether I write, read, talk, or listen,
    alert me to the power of words,
    and help me to use them wisely.
Teach me to think before I speak
    and to consider what I hear,
    that words may be a friend rather than foe,
    bringing pleasure instead of pain,
    light instead of darkness.
Amen.

40
The Convenience Store

There was no one to serve me—
   just a woman at the checkout,
   waiting to total up my bill
   and take my money.
And yes, I preferred it that way,
   for it was quick and convenient,
   giving me time to browse at leisure
   and choose as I saw fit.
Yet it made me uneasy,
   for it pointed beyond itself,
   speaking of a society
   where self-service is the norm rather than exception,
   and looking after number one the only creed.

Lord, in a world where so many cannot stand their ground;
   where the rich prosper and the poor are crushed,
   the strong thrive and the weak are backed against the wall,
   where naked self-interest
   leads to friendships being broken,
   people estranged,
   societies divided,
   and nations driven to conflict;
   teach me your way of love and humility,
   of putting the interests of others before my own.
If I would serve *you*,
   teach me to serve *all*.
Amen.

41
The Round of Drinks

It was a round of drinks,
   nothing wrong with that
   except that it was the last of many,
   and as a result one of those drinking
   would return home that night to beat his wife,
   another would brawl in the street,
   another sleep around,
   and another climb drunkenly into his car
   and mow down a passing pedestrian
   before veering off the road.

Teach us, Lord, to use rather than abuse your gifts,
   to enjoy them in moderation rather than excess.
And help us to understand that some
   must be handled with care,
   or else they will consume us instead of us them.
Amen.

42
The Stretcher

They eased him down gently,
    mindful of his wounds,
    and as they lifted and carried him
    to the waiting ambulance
    he smiled gratefully through the pain.

Thank you, Lord,
    for the knowledge that you are always there,
    ready to carry me when I cannot continue,
    to tend my wounds when I lie bruised and broken,
    to provide healing and renewal
    in body, mind, and spirit.
Teach me to minister to life's casualties in turn,
    reaching out with supportive hands and caring touch,
    in your name.
Amen.

43
The Seagull

It rose effortlessly on the breeze,
   instinctively catching the rising air—
   first this current,
   then another—
   gliding,
   swooping,
   climbing,
   diving,
   riding the thermals with casual assurance
   and exuberant delight.

Lord, release me from the chains that shackle me
   to this world,
   encumbering my mind and imprisoning my spirit.
Grant me a deeper knowledge
   of the truth that sets me free,
   that I might rise on wings of faith
   and soar in the light of your love,
   celebrating the glorious liberty your grace bestows.
Amen.

44
The Bluebell Woods

What a sight!
What a scent!
What an unforgettable picture they made!
Soon over, it's true,
    but for the month they were in bloom,
    each delicate head nodding in the breeze,
    they turned the woodland into an ocean of color
    and fragrance,
    a glimpse of Eden,
    a foretaste of paradise I will never forget.

Lord, our human span,
    like the bluebell's,
    is all too brief,
    in the context of the universe just a passing moment,
    a fleeting shadow.
Help me to make the most of the time you give me,
    living each moment to the full
    and, in my own small way,
    reflecting something of your love and glory,
    until that day when I do not merely *glimpse* paradise
    but behold it in all its glory.
Amen.

45
The Antiques Dealer

She clasped it in disbelief,
    incredulous that such a treasure
    could have been overlooked for so long,
    consigned to a crowded attic,
    and left there to gather dust,
    like so much bric-a-brac,
    so much junk.
Worthless it may have seemed to some;
    to those with eyes to see it was unique,
    priceless.

Forgive me, Lord, for overlooking the worth of others,
    seeing them as a crowd rather than individuals,
    objects instead of people.
Forgive me for dismissing what I don't understand,
    closing my eyes and ears
    to what is outside my experience
    or challenges my preconceptions.
Open my heart to the true value of all.
Amen.

46
The Injury

It was a painstaking business,
    the bones, shattered by the impact,
    needing to be pieced together like a jigsaw,
    then carefully supported
    while the breaks began to knit.
Would the injury heal,
    the body mend?
We could only hope and pray.

Lord, our world lies equally broken,
    fractured by prejudice,
    splintered by hate,
    scarred by fear,
    and for all our efforts we cannot make it whole.
Pick up the pieces and bind them together,
    bringing healing where there is hurt
    and unity where there is division.
Hear our prayer
    and honor our hopes.
Amen.

47
The Garbage Collection

They lined the streets,
    regiments of wheelie bins on their weekly parade,
    waiting to be relieved of their load
    and returned to duty.
Another day's work completed,
    another week's trash consigned to the dump.
An unglamorous business, perhaps,
    but as I watched the garbage truck on its way
    I asked myself where we'd be without it,
    what dirt, disease, and stench would take hold
    had we no such simple service.

Lord, there are all kinds of trash in my life too:
    emotional baggage and mental clutter
    that I should have discarded long ago
    but that I've allowed to build up inside,
    suffocating,
    scarring,
    polluting,
    poisoning.
Help me to recognize the litter in my life,
    the dross that disfigures and despoils,
    and teach me to dispose of it
    before it disposes of me.
Amen.

48
The Abortion Clinic

She left the clinic with a smile,
    relieved to be rid of an unwanted pregnancy,
    free once more to pursue her pleasure
    and, if another accident should occur,
    no doubt it could be fixed as easily as the last.

She left with tears in her eyes,
    forgetting the unsolicited attentions
    that had sown the seed,
    aware simply she'd said farewell to flesh of her flesh,
    bone of her bone,
    yet convinced she'd had no other choice.

She left with a groan,
    blood still oozing from her,
    haunted by what she'd done
    but haunted more by the specter
    of another mouth to feed,
    another baby to clothe,
    another child in the already overcrowded home.
No risk of that now,
    the only question, after this backstreet visit,
    whether she'd live to see tomorrow.

Some say the issue is simple, Lord,
    written in tablets of stone,
    but in this, as in so much else, I see no black or white,
    just shades of gray,
    what's right in one case seeming wrong in another.

Grant wisdom and guidance
 to all facing complex moral decisions,
 and encircle in your everlasting arms
 those whose future depends upon them.
Amen.

49
The Charity Collector

They were there outside the supermarket,
    shaking their tins hopefully,
    but I averted my eyes and shuffled past,
    pretending I hadn't noticed their presence.
I'd no loose change to salve my conscience—
    just a five-dollar bill, nothing smaller—
    so I hurried by on the other side.

Lord, forgive me,
    for I'd spent more on one treat for myself
    than the five dollars I begrudged to others.
I'd extolled the virtue of a generous heart
    yet displayed the meanest of spirits;
    my talk of concern and compassion
    exposed for the sham it was.
Teach me, next time I'm asked to give,
    to respond gladly,
    and to offer not the least I can get away with
    but more than I can truly afford.
Amen.

50
The Dictionary

What a lot of words, Lord—
   so many I can't spell,
   don't understand,
   never even knew existed:
   words for this, that, and the other,
   more than I'll use in a lifetime.

My range is more limited,
   the extent of my vocabulary puny by comparison,
   but, for all that, I'm still full of words,
   talk, as they say, coming cheap.
They have their place, of course,
   and an important one too,
   but help me, Lord, to balance them with deeds,
   putting what I say into practice.
As well as opening my mouth,
   teach me to open my heart.
Amen.

51
The Time

"Do you have the time?" he asked,
    and I was more than happy to answer,
    but though I told him the minute and hour,
    I *didn't* have the time,
    not *really*,
    not in the sense that matters most.
I'd no time for the beggar on the street corner,
    for the retiree struggling with her shopping,
    or for the student distributing the flyers;
    no time to write that letter,
    make that phone call,
    or visit that lonely neighbor;
    no time to get involved with the local cause,
    respond to the national campaign,
    support the global charity;
    no time to relax,
    unwind,
    or take stock;
    no time, in fact, for anything but chasing my tail.

Lord, despite my rushing around in circles,
    I could achieve far more
    if only I were to get my priorities right
    and focus on the things that matter.
So little of what I do is as pressing as I think
    and so much gets me nowhere.
Teach me to *make* time—
    for me, for others,
    and for you.
Amen.

52
The Cul-De-Sac

There'd been no sign,
   no warning—
   one moment it was like any other street
   and the next it just petered out:
   a dead end,
   a road to nowhere.

Lord,
   my life feels like that sometimes.
I stride out confidently,
   believing I know the best way forward,
   only to be pulled up short,
   stopped in my tracks by some disappointment,
   problem, or tragedy,
   and I'm left asking, "What now?"
   "Why am I here?"
   "Where next?"

Speak to me, Lord,
   when life seems bereft of meaning and purpose.
Direct my steps,
   give light to my path,
   and lead me in your eternal way.
Amen.

53
The AIDS Sufferer

They avoided him,
    shrinking back when he approached,
    well aware the response was foolish,
    but controlled by half-formed fears,
    suspicion and prejudice like a wall between them.
No comment was made—
    none was needed:
    he walked forlornly away,
    condemned to carry his burden alone.

Some say it's a punishment, Lord,
    a sign of your anger.
Others pity him.
Most keep their distance.
But not you.
As you touched the untouchables
    throughout your ministry,
    so you reach out still,
    seeing not the affliction
    but the person underneath.
Forgive, Lord, the feebleness of our love,
    and teach us to do the same.
Amen.

54
The Rechargeable Battery

It was dead,
   no use to anyone,
   but that, of course, was soon put right.
A quick charge
   and it was as good as new,
   ready for action,
   energy restored.

Lord, I too feel drained sometimes,
   fit for nothing,
   reserves run dry.
Yet you are a God of power,
   revitalizing the spirit,
   renewing strength.
Flow into my heart,
   and out through my life.
Amen.

55
The Pebble

It was perfectly smooth,
    the fissures and fractures it had once held
    long since worn away by the pounding of waves
    and ceaseless jostling of its fellows,
    each stone helping to round the next.

Lord, I too need the company of others
    to remove rough edges,
    the experience of rubbing shoulders
    with people of different backgrounds,
    ideas, and experiences
    if I'm to become fully rounded.
Open my heart to others,
    and through my bouncing off them
    shape my life for good.
Amen.

56
The Breeze

It caressed my cheek,
   gentle and soothing,
   offering welcome relief
   from the heat of the noontime sun,
   and then it was gone to who knows where.
What stories could it tell?
What places had it seen?
What forms taken,
   lives touched,
   paths followed?
Had it raged in a tropical storm,
   whipped up desert sand,
   or whistled over polar ice sheets?
Had it sped sailors across the ocean,
   lifted eagles high above mountain peaks,
   sent leaves cascading from bronze-leafed woodland?
Or was this the start of a new journey,
   the tranquil air stirring from silent slumber
   to wild wakefulness?

Lord, remind me
   that I can no more fathom the workings of your mind
   than control the course of the wind;
   that I can never know, still less dictate,
   where and when you will move,
   or in what ways and among whom
   you may choose to act.
Open my life to whatever you would do,
   wherever, whenever, and however you choose to do it.
Amen.

57
The Text Message

He texted me—
    nothing eloquent or fancy,
    just a simple message to stay in touch,
    a quick word to keep me in the picture,
    reinforcing the friendship we'd built up over the years.

Lord, teach us that staying in touch with you
    doesn't require special language
    or a formal approach,
    but is about a living relationship,
    making time to share every aspect of life—
    from the momentous to the mundane,
    the agony and ecstasy,
    triumphs and tribulations—
    each shared simply but sincerely
    in the knowledge that they matter to you
    because *we* matter.
Amen.

58
The Baby

I held her, Lord,
   that tiny life,
   so vulnerable and dependent,
   yet so full of promise,
   cradled in my arms.
Who could say what the future might hold,
   what adventures and achievements might lie ahead?
Life was a blank canvas,
   the details yet even to be sketched.

Lord, for me such freshness is a distant memory,
   the portrait of my life all but drawn,
   days as much now about memories as anticipation,
   about what *was* as what yet might be.
Yet that is to forget
   the fresh start you daily make possible.
Rekindle in me the flame of hope
   and fire of expectancy,
   in the knowledge that, with you,
   however old we might be,
   life has always only just begun.
Amen.

59
The Toddler

He was into everything—
    impatient,
    inquisitive,
    incorrigible—
    and though he needed the occasional restraining hand,
    I'd have had it no other way.
He was eager to explore,
    thirsting for knowledge,
    conscious of so much still to be discovered
    and understood.

Lord, give me that same desire in terms of faith—
    a resolve to grow in commitment,
    develop in understanding,
    and mature in discipleship.
Keep me young in spirit,
    childlike in my appetite for life
    and ever-youthful in my hunger
    to learn more of the world
    and more of you.
Amen.

60
The Discarded Lottery Ticket

I found it in the street,
   trodden into the dust
   like the hopes of the one who'd bought it,
   and it set me thinking
   of the hundreds, thousands, millions who,
   week after week,
   fritter away a few more dollars
   in pursuit of their dream—
   an escape from the daily grind,
   and, in its place, a taste of the good life,
   comfort and contentment guaranteed.

Teach me, Lord, that true happiness is not a lottery
   but a gift;
   not dependent on wealth or possessions
   but freely available to all;
   not rooted on earth
   but kept in heaven,
   to be tasted now
   and savored for all eternity.
Teach me to celebrate each day as it comes,
   rejoicing in all you have lavished upon me
   and anticipating the treasures yet held in store.
Amen.

61
The Advertisements

It was laughable, really,
    the claims more exaggerated by the day:
    new,
    enhanced,
    improved;
    the most advanced formula ever,
    the finest and fastest of its kind;
    great value,
    great quality,
    great everything—
    quite simply, the best that money could buy.

Lord, I make extravagant claims—
    about the way you've changed my life,
    the person you've helped me become,
    and the life you've called me to lead.
Forgive me when the walk denies the talk,
    what people see in me
        leading them to dismiss the faith I profess
    as empty hype,
    more spin than substance.
Work within me,
    so that who I am may more closely resemble
    who you want me to be.
Amen.

62
The Fisherman

He'd been there for hours,
   sprawled on the bank,
   occasionally stirring to reel in his line
   and bait his hook afresh.
No rush,
   no bustle—
   seemingly all the time in the world.
But then,
   suddenly,
   a nibble,
   a tug on the line
   and he was up,
   hauling in his catch—
   another successful day's fishing.

Lord, I'm not good at waiting.
I like to see speedy results,
   instant returns,
   and when plans are frustrated,
   rewards delayed,
   I fret and sulk.
I'm not good at waiting for *you* either,
   angry when prayers go unanswered,
   requests apparently unheeded.
Remind me that the best things come to those who wait,
   and teach me to do things not in *my* time,
   but *yours*.
Amen.

63
The Supermarket

Food, drink, clothes, books;
    houseware, electrical goods, even insurance—
    all there under one roof at bargain prices,
    everything we needed,
    all we could ask for.
And crowds flocked accordingly
    to this consumer paradise,
    a cathedral of delights.

I'm not knocking it, Lord,
    for the bargains are welcome,
    the selection excellent,
    and the convenience a bonus,
    but I can stack my cart full,
    yet still leave empty,
    if I imagine what I buy can meet my needs.
It may feed the body
    but not the soul,
    delight the senses
    but not the spirit—
    contentment being a gift rather than a product,
    a treasure to be received
    rather than a commodity plucked from a shelf.
Teach me where true fulfillment lies,
    and to seek it before all else.
Amen.

64
The Oak Tree

It stood solid and strong,
   its gnarled and knotted roots
   protruding through the ground like swollen veins,
   sustaining the life that coursed
   through the mighty trunk and twisted branches.
Through wind, rain, drought, and frost,
   it had stood defiant,
   its vigor undiminished,
   and no doubt it will see out centuries to come,
   as it has centuries gone by.

Lord, anchor my life in your love,
   your word,
   your will,
   that I too may be able to resist
   the trials life throws at me.
Nurture my faith and strengthen my commitment,
   so that whatever turmoil I face,
   whatever testing endure,
   when all has done its worst
   I may still stand tall—
   unbowed,
   unbroken.
Amen.

65
The Politician

They were fine policies, I'll give him that,
    and possibly,
        behind the electioneering, rhetoric, and spin,
    he meant what he said.
But I'd seen it all before,
    too many times to number—
    what's pledged now reneged on later,
    an excuse always found for failing to deliver,
    for diluting those solemn vows.

Teach me, Lord, that you are different,
    your word constant,
    your promise sure,
    your faithfulness certain.
Though all else may disappoint,
    remind me that you will not.
Amen.

66
The eBay Auction

They waited before making their bids,
    each anxious to pay as little as possible
    to secure their prize,
    and then, as the price rose,
    one by one
    they fell away,
    the cost too high to stomach.

With you, Lord, it's a different story.
Though I am worth so little,
    you were willing to give your all,
    gladly and without reserve,
    no price too high or cost too great
    to make me yours
    and you mine.
For that awesome truth
    and amazing love,
    thank you.
Amen.

67
The Footprints

They snaked ahead of me,
    footprints in the snow,
    a welcome sign
    that someone had walked that way before me
    and made it through.
Whose they were I would never know,
    but they spurred me on,
    giving me heart to continue
    where I would otherwise have turned back.

Thank you, Lord, for those who have walked your way,
    leaving footsteps for me to follow.
Whatever obstacles I may face,
    teach me to stay true to the path in turn,
    so that I too, in some small way,
    may inspire others as they journey in faith.
Amen.

68
The Meal

They ate dutifully enough,
   smiling politely
   and making the odd appreciative noise,
   but I knew they were enjoying it no more than I was.
The meal was bland,
   all but tasteless,
   and with good reason,
   for I'd forgotten to add seasoning—
   so small an ingredient,
   so large an effect.

Forgive me, Lord, for the insipid fare I offer you,
   looking the part
   and with so many of the components right,
   yet lacking the one thing needful:
   the savor of love.
Teach me that the poorest of dishes
   with that one vital ingredient
   is worth far more than the finest of feasts without it.
Amen.

69
The Computer Scan

I scanned my computer today,
   a routine check for problems,
   and watched aghast as the list grew:
   viruses,
   bugs,
   spyware,
   spam—
   so much that had crept in unnoticed,
   insidiously infiltrating my system,
   corrupting,
   infecting,
   destroying.

Examine me, Lord, and know my heart.
Test me and search my thoughts.
Delve deep within
   and cleanse me from all that fragments my faith
   and undermines my commitment,
   preventing me from living as you intend.
Reformat,
   renew,
   restore.
Amen.

70
The Tide

It was a sea of mud now,
>haven to a host of waders probing for tasty tidbits,
>a bleak and desolate expanse,
>haunting and mournful.

Yet already the tide was turning,
>the scene soon to be a sea of blue once more,
>shimmering in the sunlight,
>splashing on the shore,
>a haven for boats bobbing on the swell
>and children paddling among the waves.

Day in, day out,
>like a gentle pulse,
>it rises and falls,
>ebbs and flows.

For me too, Lord, life brings its ups and downs.
Remind me that they belong together,
>each a part of the greater whole,
>and teach me to trust you
>through both the highs and lows,
>sensing through it all the rhythm of your grace
>and heartbeat of your love.

Amen.

71
The Vacation

I needed that break,
   more than I realized,
   for in the bustle of each day
   I'd lost touch with the simple but special things in life.
I had time, suddenly, to stop, stare, pause, and ponder –
   to appreciate flowers in bloom and birds in song,
   the scent of the sea and caress of the breeze,
   uplifting the heart and soothing the spirit,
   gifts beyond price.

Teach me, Lord, whatever else needs doing,
   to make time to unwind and hear your voice,
   to be still and glimpse your presence.
Save me from being so concerned
   with the daily demands of life
   that I have no time left truly to live.
Amen.

72
The Street Cleaner

Day after day he trod the streets,
   unnoticed by many,
   unappreciated by most,
   his work dull,
   dirty,
   even demeaning,
   but important for all.

Lord, the tasks you call us to may not be glamorous,
   catching the eye or earning the plaudits,
   but they are no less necessary for that,
   for so often it is those in the shadows
   who are the unsung heroes,
   support staff who make possible the star roles.
Grant us, then, humility
   to serve in whatever way you ask,
   and to appreciate the ways *others* serve *us*.
Amen.

73
The Muslim

He sat in the subway train,
    aware of the eyes turned on him—
    inquisitive eyes, intrigued by his appearance,
    suspicious eyes, fearful of some hidden agenda,
    hostile eyes, resentful at his presence—
    so many eyes failing to see behind the labels
    or below the surface
    to the person underneath.

Forgive me, Lord, for the way I too pigeonhole people,
    unconsciously absorbing the prejudices of society
    even as I resist them,
    shaped by fears and preconceptions
    I'm not even aware of,
    hiding behind generalizations that say more about
    me than others.
Open my eyes to see people as they are,
    rather than as I construe them to be.
Amen.

74
The Calculator

He tapped in the numbers, one after the other,
   and came up with the right result,
   down to the tenth decimal point,
   but he'd little idea how he'd got there,
   his grasp of mathematics minimal.
Having never grasped the essentials for himself,
   stripped of the calculator he'd be lost.

Lord, in terms of Christian belief
   I can come up with the right answers,
   but unless I've experienced the truth for myself
   that counts for little.
Teach me to know you personally
   instead of relying on the perception of others;
   to work *out* my faith
   and *at* my discipleship,
   so that it all makes sense for *me*.
Amen.

75
The Space Probe

They were exciting pictures—
    fascinating glimpses of swirling gas,
    soaring mountains,
    massive craters,
    and rocky wastes.
At last we knew a little more about the universe beyond,
    but it was simply a single planet,
    one of trillions spiraling away into infinity;
    in terms of our solar system,
    let alone space,
    just a stone's throw away.
For all it taught us,
    the lesson brought home was how vast are the heavens
    and how small is the earth.

Thank you, Lord, for the capacity of humankind
    to explore profound mysteries,
    for our ability constantly to push back the boundaries
    of comprehension.
But thank you also for your incomparable greatness—
    the unfathomable immensity of your love,
    awesome breadth of your purpose,
    and staggering scale of your power.
You are higher than our highest thoughts,
    above all, before all, and beyond all.
Receive my praise.
Amen.

76
The New Home

It was an unsettling few months—
    weighing up the pros and cons,
    checking the bank balance,
    viewing properties,
    packing belongings—
    but at last it was done,
    contracts exchanged and keys handed over.
Yet we still had our doubts,
    on the one hand, excited,
    on the other, fearful.
Would the neighbors be OK,
    the roof leak,
    the double-glazing need replacing?
Would the policy cover the mortgage,
    interest rates stay low,
    the market keep on rising?
Time alone would tell.

Lord, you promise us another home,
    not made with human hands but kept in heaven,
    a house with many rooms,
    where we will dwell in the light of your love
    forevermore.
I'm not sure of the details—
    where or when it will be,
    or what form life will take there—
    but that's not important,
    for you tell me all I need to know.
Time indeed *will* tell.
Amen.

77
The Moving Truck

It came as a shock:
   box upon box,
   crate after crate,
   a mountain of possessions I barely knew I had.
They'd built up over the years—
   stuffed into closets,
   stashed into drawers,
   or simply piled high in the shed, attic, garage—
   and though I'd had the occasional sift through,
   they'd accumulated faster than I could dispose of them,
   until they filled almost every nook and cranny.

Lord, I mean to focus on treasures in heaven,
   but the lure of earthly goods is so strong
   that I buy first this, then that,
   until the shelves groan
   and cupboards creak under their weight,
   and the irony, Lord, is that they hang heavy on me too,
   becoming a burden rather than blessing,
   encumbrance rather than asset.
Teach me to let go of the clutter that ties me to earth,
   so that my spirit might soar unfettered,
   truly free.
Amen.

78
The Sunglasses

They shielded my eyes from the worst of the glare,
   allowing me to gaze for a moment at the setting sun
   and glimpse its glory,
   a golden ball of light.
Without them I was dazzled,
   the light too much to bear,
   forcing me to look away.

Before you also, Lord, I must turn aside,
   your splendor too intense,
   your brightness too awesome,
   and yet, through Christ, I glimpse your glory,
   wonderful beyond words.
For now it is partial,
   as though I look through darkened glasses,
   but it is enough and more than enough
   to lighten my path
   and illuminate my soul.
Shine now,
   shine always,
   through his radiant love.
Amen.

79
The Movie Theater

They watched enthralled,
    transported to another world,
    sharing the pain and passion of those on screen,
    eyes now bright,
    now wide with fear,
    now filled with tears.
But then it ended—
    the spell broken,
    characters left behind—
    and they returned to the reassuring world of reality,
    the scenes that had so recently engrossed them
    soon forgotten,
    left behind.

Lord, I see other scenes day after day,
    news pictures of hunger, squalor, violence, and suffering
    beamed into my living room from across the world,
    and my heart goes out to those enduring such misery.
But once more I can walk away,
    leaving it all behind.
Only there's no such leaving for them:
    this is *their* reality.
Remind me, Lord, that these are real people,
    each one my neighbor,
    and instead of pushing them aside,
    as if they are part of another world,
    teach me, whenever and wherever I can,
    to respond in love.
Amen.

80
The Accident

An accident, they called it,
   but it wasn't.
The car was going too fast,
   the driver absorbed in conversation,
   not looking,
   not thinking,
   not focused on the task in hand.
And the result was a father stretched out in the morgue,
   a mother fighting for her life,
   a child who would never walk again,
   and a toddler hideously scarred.

Lord, I'd never hurt anyone on purpose,
   yet I *do* hurt them, too many times to number,
   wounding the spirit if not the body.
A foolish comment here,
   thoughtless deed there,
   and before I know it the harm is done—
   what seems innocuous capable of wreaking havoc.
Save me, Lord, from hasty words and careless actions,
   and in all I say or do
   teach me to consider others
   and to consider you.
Amen.

81
The Military Graves

It was peaceful,
   almost pastoral,
   the gravestones standing neatly to attention,
   row upon row
   stretching across the crisply mowed lawns.
But the stillness and order belied the truth,
   masking the turmoil that had scarred those fields,
   the slaughter and sacrifice,
   fear and despair—
   each name a loved one plucked away,
   each stone a memorial to broken lives
   and shattered dreams,
   stark testimony to the horror yet heroism of war,
   the price paid,
   and debt owed.

Teach me, Lord, truly to appreciate the freedom I enjoy
   and never to forget what it cost so many.
Remind me of the awfulness of conflict,
   that I might strive always for peace.
And awaken me to my part in a broken world
   and my responsibility to work for its healing.
Amen.

82
The Credit Card Statement

It was there in black and white,
  chilling,
  inescapable.
He'd spent more than he realized,
  more than he could afford,
  and was left now with a debt around his neck,
  an amount owing that would take months,
  even years,
  to repay.

Lord, I can never earn your love,
  still less repay your goodness toward me,
  but you do not ask me to.
You have canceled the debt,
  writing it off as though it had never been.
Though I owe so much,
  you ask me simply to receive.
Though I deserve so little,
  you offer new life in Christ,
  free and overflowing.
For the awesome generosity of your gift,
  Lord, I thank you.
Amen.

83
The Door

He knocked and knocked again,
   but there was no answer;
   the door firmly closed,
   denying entry.
Was there no one at home?
Were his knocks unheard?
Or was his presence ignored,
   his company unwelcome?

Lord,
   forgive me for closing the door to you,
   repeatedly denying you access into my life.
Forgive me for shutting you out
   when your presence unsettles
   and your word confronts,
   when you ask questions of me I would rather not face
   and make demands I prefer to avoid.
Open my heart to your love,
   my mind to your truth,
   and my soul to your grace,
   so that you might live in me
   and I in you.
Amen.

84
The Footpath

It had been easy at first,
    a waymarked path winding away into the distance,
    and I'd set off confidently,
    striding out in eager expectation.
But then the track narrowed—
    strewn with nettles and choked by thorns,
    hard sometimes to follow,
    hard even to find—
    until finally I turned back,
    taking the road instead,
    less fulfilling perhaps,
    but less demanding for sure.

Lord, it seemed easy at first, walking your way,
    the path clear,
    the journey simple,
    but slowly the going grew harder,
    the trail obscure,
    until finally I lost heart and turned back,
    preferring the wide and inviting way of the world
    that promises much and asks little.
Yet though that path is easier, it leads to nowhere.
Guide my footsteps
    and give me strength
    to finish the journey of discipleship,
    however challenging the route may be.
Amen.

85
The Hall of Mirrors

We laughed together,
    for the images were grotesque,
    hideously distorted—
    our legs like matchsticks,
    chests like tree trunks,
    faces stretched and figures squashed
    beyond recognition—
    a travesty of the truth.
It was funny because it was phoney,
    each reflection an intended caricature,
    a distortion of reality.

What do people see in me, Lord,
    beneath the mask of piety
    and veneer of commitment?
What picture do I give them?
What image convey of you?
Forgive me,
    for I see now, in a rare moment of honesty,
    the false and flawed reflection I offer,
    and I'm laughing no longer,
    for it's another caricature,
    as gross as the other,
    only this time there's no mirror;
    it's all too real.
Amen.

86
The Fountain

It danced in the breeze,
    a cascade of water leaping and cavorting,
    like a newborn lamb,
    a playful kitten,
    exuberant,
    free,
    full of life.
Restless and vivacious,
    it spoke of unquenchable energy,
    an irrepressible vitality bubbling deep within.

May your Spirit, Lord, course through me
    with similar energy,
    your joy with comparable verve,
    your love with equal spontaneity,
    and your peace with matching abandon.
So fill me with your presence,
    that my soul may dance each day
    in jubilant praise and exultant gratitude.
Amen.

87
The Ruler

It was a simple enough task—
  to draw a straight line
  of a certain length
  in an exact place—
  yet without that ruler, I'd have struggled,
  unable to get my bearings,
  take measurements,
  or keep on track.

Without you, Lord, I struggle too,
  less than straight in my dealings with others,
  hesitant in following my intended course,
  unable to draw a line under the past,
  incapable of measuring up to the call of Christ.
Open my heart to the height, length, and depth
  of your loving purpose,
  and may that yardstick
  bring new dimensions to life each day
  and a proper perspective on all I do.
Amen.

88
The Stain

I tried everything—
   rinsing, rubbing,
   soaking, scrubbing—
   but to no avail.
It was still there,
   an ugly stain,
   impossible to miss,
   hard to ignore.

The blots in my life, Lord, are equally unsightly,
   too many to number,
   too many to hide.
I strive in vain to remove them,
   to conquer their hold or conceal their presence,
   but try as I might they still show through.
Take what I am, Lord—
   with all the dirt that sticks so closely,
   the ingrained grime that stains my soul—
   and, by your grace, wash me,
   and make me clean.
Amen.

89
The Shoelaces

Don't ask me how,
    but they were knotted again,
    twisted into a hopeless tangle,
    and the more I tugged and teased
    the more tightly snarled they became,
    impossible to unravel.

I get into a similar mess, Lord,
    struggling to make sense of life
    or to extricate myself from the tangled web I weave.
I search for answers to my questions,
    solutions to my problems,
    but the harder I try to disentangle the loose ends,
    the more tightly I tie myself in knots.
Meet me in my confusion,
    and gather the jumbled threads of my life together.
Entwine them with the cords of your love,
    creating there,
    and there alone,
    a bond that can never be loosened.
Amen.

90
The Chapel of Rest

He was so still,
   so quiet,
   lying there like a marble statue—
   cold,
   impassive,
   no longer the person I knew
   but an empty shell,
   like a casket stripped of its treasure,
   a house with no one at home,
   and I grieved for the one I had lost.

Lord, I need to grieve,
   for the sorrow is real,
   the pain hard to bear,
   but I also need to rejoice,
   for with you death is not the end
   but a new beginning.
The shell is empty but has nurtured life.
The casket is bare but its treasure safe in your hands.
The person I knew I will know again,
   for he is truly at home,
   secure in your everlasting arms,
   alive with all your people,
   forevermore.
Amen.

91
The Bananas

There were hundreds of them,
    bunch upon bunch
    piled high on the supermarket shelf,
    and, with barely a second thought,
    a succession of shoppers grabbed a handful,
    pausing only to check the quality
    before adding some to their shopping cart.

I know, Lord, for I was one of them,
    eagerly filling my basket in turn,
    yet in each bunch,
    had I ears to hear,
    you were speaking:
    of justice and injustice,
    trade and commerce,
    toil and effort,
    sweat and tears—
    of the interdependence of humankind
    and the complex web of life.
Remind me each day of what I owe to others,
    near and far,
    and the many ways they enrich my life.
Remind me of the breadth and wonder of creation
    and my responsibilities toward all.
Amen.

92
The Storm Clouds

They changed everything, those clouds, in an instant—
  one moment the world bathed in light
  and the next a shadow over all,
  one moment full of warmth
  and the next a brooding chill.
Thunder rumbled,
  lightning streaked the sky,
  and the storm broke in wild fury . . .
  and then it was gone,
  skies bright once more,
  threat replaced by promise,
  sunshine after rain.

Remind me, Lord, in the storms of life,
  when the clouds hang heavy
  and the world seems dark,
  that your light continues to shine
  though all seems in turmoil.
Teach me, however distant you may seem,
  still to trust you,
  assured that your love will break through
  and its radiance enfold me once more.
Amen.

93
The Ecstasy Tablet

It looked harmless enough,
    more like a sweet than a drug,
    and though it cost rather more
    it was being handed out like Smarties.
Let your hair down, was the message,
    relax, live a little.
Why not?
Everyone else is.
But as they stumbled home, bleary-eyed,
    the cold light of day returning,
    did they spare a thought for the girl in intensive care,
    poisoned by the adulterated tablet;
    for the elderly woman mugged of her savings
    to pay for the growing addiction;
    for the youngsters moving on to crack cocaine;
    for the hallucinating child,
    the boy waking up to black depression,
    or the teenager thrown into a fit?

Reach out, Lord, to all who,
    seeking freedom and fulfillment,
    abuse their bodies to escape them;
    all who, in their search for happiness,
    are vulnerable to unscrupulous predators.
Help them to get a buzz out of life
    not through artificial means,
    chemically induced elation,
    but through experiencing the thrill of your presence,
    and tasting the inner ecstasy that you alone can bring.
Amen.

94
The Medicine

She gulped it down hurriedly,
   screwing up her face in disgust,
   the taste far from her liking,
   but she knew it was needed,
   vital if she was to get well,
   so she opened her mouth again,
   reluctant but dutiful,
   and accepted the full dose.

Lord, you ask me sometimes to take *my* medicine,
   unwelcome though it might be:
   to face up to the consequences of my actions,
   pay the price of some folly,
   swallow my pride,
   learn my lesson,
   pay my dues.
I don't enjoy it any more than the next person,
   but help me at such times
   to remember it's for my own good,
   the prescription designed to heal, not hurt,
   correct rather than castigate,
   discipline instead of punish.
Though I do not relish the treatment,
   use it to make me whole.
Amen.

95
The Surfers

I watched them riding the waves,
    their exhilaration plain
    as, in glorious harmony with the elements,
    they ducked, dived, twisted, and turned,
    and I marvelled at the beauty and grandeur of creation,
    its power to uplift the body and transport the spirit,
    wonderful beyond words.
But I couldn't help recalling other waves,
    destructive
    terrifying,
    engulfing homes,
    obliterating communities—
    a merciless torrent overwhelming countless lives—
    and I marvelled at the savagery of creation,
    its power to *crush* the body and *shatter* the spirit,
    dreadful beyond words.

Why, Lord, did you create a world so awesome
    yet so awful,
    enriched by joy yet cursed by sorrow;
    a world in which so much speaks of your care,
    but so much else denies it,
    giving your love the lie?
Help me to wrestle honestly with the good and bad,
    the best and the worst in life,
    and somehow to make sense of you in each.
Amen.

96
The Jigsaw Puzzle

There was a piece missing!
After all the effort I'd put in,
   the painstaking hours of concentration,
   I was left frustrated,
   dismayed,
   for the puzzle was incomplete.
Hard though I looked,
   long though I searched,
   it proved in vain,
   the picture, it seemed,
   condemned to remain unfinished.

For many, Lord, it's not a puzzle that's incomplete
   but life itself.
For all their striving, they feel unfulfilled,
   a component missing,
   and though they can't quite place what it is,
   they search hungrily for that special something,
   that elusive final piece to complete the picture.
Draw near to them,
   that in you they may find what they seek:
   the One who satisfies our inner yearning,
   and gives meaning to all.
Amen.

97
The Bridge

It spanned the divide,
  allowing passage between the two,
  those formerly separated suddenly brought close,
  the gulf skillfully bridged.

Lord, in a divided world,
  where chasms of fear, hatred, envy, and injustice
  come between so many,
  help me to build bridges—
  to do what I can,
  where I can,
  to construct links,
  create dialogue
  and promote partnership,
  bringing together those previously kept apart.
Where barriers estrange and rifts alienate,
  help me to be a peacemaker.
Amen.

98
The Swimming Lesson

I was scared, Lord,
    scared of lifting my feet off the bottom
    and trusting myself to the water.
I knew what I had to do,
    and could see others around me doing it—
    the thought of going under
    never even entering their heads.
But theory was one thing,
    practice another.
It needed a leap of faith,
    and I was afraid to make it.

Lord, I don't find faith in *you* any easier.
Though I talk blithely enough about it,
    when it comes to the moment of truth,
    to letting go and trusting you,
    I'm as nervous as a kitten,
    testing the water but no more,
    and thus failing either to sink or swim.
Give me the courage I need to take the plunge
    and place my all in your hands.
Amen.

99
The Wrong Note

It was unmistakable,
    a dissonant note blaring out above the others,
    harsh and grating,
    destroying the mood in a moment,
    shattering the harmony.

Lord, you do not expect me
    always to be in concert with others,
    in unison with their every whim and wish,
    for there are times when faithful discipleship
    entails singing to a different tune,
    and clashes are inevitable,
    but help me to avoid what inevitably leads to discord—
    pride,
    hatred,
    deceit,
    envy,
    selfishness,
    anger,
    greed.
Help me to strike the right note at the right time,
    as far as possible living harmoniously with all.
Amen.

100
The Ornament

It was an attractive piece, there's no denying it—
   not just any old doily,
   but carefully crafted,
   artistic and elegant,
   yet it had no purpose other than to enhance the décor,
   filling an otherwise empty space.
It was for show only,
   intentionally so,
   its function simply to please the eye.

Lord, I know appearances matter,
   but you call me to practical commitment
   rather than ornamental discipleship,
   to a faith that makes a difference.
Save me from showy discipleship
   that's more froth than substance.
Show me what you would have me do
   and help me to do it,
   that I may be not only pleasing in your sight
   but also useful in your service.
Amen.

www.ingramcontent.com/pod-product-compliance
Lightning Source LLC
Chambersburg PA
CBHW071215070526
44584CB00019B/3034